The Non-Guide to the No-Thing

VOLUME TWO

A Simple, Clear Explanation of
What the 'Paradigm Shift' Actually Means

TERRY FAVOUR

AMADO PRESS
AMADO, ARIZONA

To Charlie and Debbie,
my very own constituency
of dedicated thinkers

Introduction

I wrote this second volume because as my own understanding of this unfathomable subject deepened, I became astonished at the amount of information available to us from our own Western traditions. Like many others, I had looked to Eastern spiritual traditions for the much-needed guidance that seemed so lacking here in the West.

The truth that is the result of the past 3,000 years of concentrated effort has just in the last 100 years come to fruition. Because this fruition has just come about, and, because most of the people responsible for it do not themselves understand what has transpired, this magnificent culmination has gone unnoticed.

In fact, in the 3,000 years it took to accomplish this tremendous feat, we actually forgot what it was we were searching for in the first place. No wonder we don't recognize the result.

We forgot that when we began this quest for knowledge, we were asking, "Who are we?" But as we approached the scientific revolution, the quest became about our own power. Francis Bacon, who was so influential in bringing about the scientific revolution, made it clear that the only knowledge that is not "mere trifling" is the knowledge that enables us to make nature do our bidding. In spite of that, using the fantastic technology that Bacon aspired to, we have stayed on course, as our Greek forefathers would have wished. And we have answered the question, "Who are we?"

As yet, most of us don't realize this. But one man, living almost the entire span of the 20th century, was very clear about this all-encompassing Western adventure. His name was Owen Barfield. We sometimes hear about him in conjunction with his friends, C.S. Lewis and J.R.R. Tolkien. Owen Barfield was a linguist who made his discoveries about our Western quest from that discipline. He wrote the book *Saving the Appearances*, which, though it is beautifully written, is difficult to read. Despite the difficult reading, his succinct and brilliant overview of our Western evolution of consciousness makes his book one of the most important to date. While I have not written this little volume strictly from his point of view, it was primarily written in an effort to make his great work more accessible.

In no way should this book take the place of *Saving the Appearances*. It should be regarded as a kind of groundbreaker for those who are interested in pursuing further what I believe to be the end of an era and the beginning of a new one. This era could be the beginning of the most unimaginable and exciting adventure ever dreamed of.

Paradigm Review

In Volume 1, we acknowledged
that our solid-looking world is not solid.
We followed the cutting edge of Western
science to quantum physics and the discovery
that things, at their core, have no real
material substance.

We discovered that if this quantum
view is the true foundation of our world, then
our human bodies, at the core, are not made
of any real substance either.

If we are not material substance,
what are we? Volume 1 came to the conclusion
that we are actually AWARENESS. We are the
awareness that the forms of the material
world appear to be solid WITHIN.

Let's try to uncover what not being material substance really means, and therefore, how the experiences of our daily lives actually happen.

The focus of our attention creates our reality by including some things and at the same time excluding other things. Our focus of attention continually creates limits. The very definition of form includes the idea of limits. Without limits we are faced with undifferentiated potential, with waves and particles, and with the realm of infinite possibilities.

If this is true, how do things get to be things? In other words, how do waves/particles become form? How do they get to be familiar objects?

D o things exist as solid matter if they
go unnoticed? Do things exist independent of US?
Is there some interrelatedness between what appears
to be solid matter and OUR senses and OUR minds?

In very simplified terms, quantum physics (which studies the very small), says that a wave equals potential until it is observed. Only when a wave is observed does it go from potential to actual, from a wave to a particle.

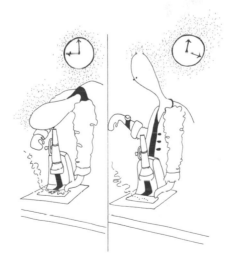

Focus of Attention

To make this clear, we need an analogy. Consider the rainbow. Does a rainbow exist independent of its observer?

Think of all you know about a rainbow.
For a rainbow to exist, three ingredients must
be present. There must be sun, raindrops and, of course,
the vision of the observer. In other words, a rainbow's
existence depends on the actual optical apparatus of
the eye. It is that apparatus that puts the sun and the
raindrops together, forming the 'vision' of the rainbow.

E ven so, I still can't touch the rainbow.
If I try to walk to the end of it, it won't be there.
But if a friend observes it with me, she will see it
too, and we will agree that it does exist.

The we must consider this. Is it true that as soon as anyone sees a rainbow it therefore exists? If so, what is a hallucination or the vision of a madman? Would you believe a person who claimed to have seen a rainbow on a sunless or cloudless day?

F or us to know that a rainbow is actually there, there must be sun, raindrops and the observer's vision. And somehow the observer's mind is also involved. There must be collective agreement about the existence of rainbows, as well. But let's not go too fast. We will investigate this further as we go along.

Take the rainbow example and apply it
to a table. Like the rainbow, we can see a table. But
unlike the rainbow, we can also touch a table. It makes
a sound if we hit it. If it is made of wood, it could
burn and then we would smell it too.

Unlike the rainbow, our senses tell us
that a table is made of solid matter. Just as you
did with the rainbow, think of all you know about
a table—which appears to be made of solid matter.

We have considered the effect an observer
has upon waves, and that in the realm of the very
tiny, waves actually become particles when observed.
Matter is composed of particles. The table appears
to be made of solid matter.

But NOW we know that even a table is
not solid. What actually makes up the table is what
I have been calling particles: waves that have become
particles upon observation, particles that have interacted
with sense perception and then become the table. Neither
the raindrops nor the particles of the table are like what
they become. Just as the rainbow is the outcome of the
raindrops and my vision, a table is the outcome of the
particles, my vision and my other senses. And now it
is time to bring the mind's role into this.

To explain how the mind fits in, imagine
a situation. One morning as you awaken, the room
you are in and its furnishings are just coming into focus.
You notice it all, including a table. You don't know exactly
where you are. You recognize objects in the room but they
seem totally unfamiliar. You realize that you are NOT in
your bedroom at home! Suddenly you remember that
you have been traveling. You remember where you are.
In an instant everything snaps into place. The room
suddenly has context and looks familiar.

What happens though, when something appears to the senses for which the mind has no context— collective or personal? For example, have you heard the story that when the first European ships sailed into the harbor of some primitive island, the natives could not see the ships at all? The ships were outside their experience, and therefore outside the perception of their senses.

How does this tie into the first volume
of *The Non-Guide to the No-Thing* and the
paradigm change it disclosed?

Then / Now

When humanity agrees collectively about what is real and what is not real about the world, then we have a paradigm. When, in time, that view changes, and the human agreement changes, as it has many many times, then the world changes too.

Just how far does this collective agreement go? Would there be form at all if there were not a sensate being with a conscious mind? These volumes propose that there cannot be form as we know it without human observation, since the manifested and the unmanifested are different aspects of the same thing. And what of collective agreement? If we all agree on what is real and what is not, have we not shown that our concept of reality IS our agreement? Do we not call this agreement FACT? Once it was FACT that the world was flat.

If the collective agreement changes, then
the form actually changes. This can be quite radical.
But once the change has occurred, the past paradigm passes
out of experience to such a degree that the true meaning
of the prior view is lost. It becomes inaccessible, since
it is not WITHIN the particular confines of
our current view.

This is our predicament today. Something happened about 500-600 years ago that radically changed our paradigm, but we have no memory of how we actually viewed the world before that change. The limitations of our current collective agreement lock us out.

Two things happened over time about 500-600 years ago. One was the invention of the printing press, which spread the written word. The other was the scientific revolution. In order to better understand these changes, I introduce the use of three words in a particular way.

Three Words

Alpha-thinking

Figuration

Beta-thinking

The three words, originally proposed by linguist Owen Barfield in *Saving the Appearances*, are: alpha-thinking, beta-thinking, and most important, figuration.

Alpha-thinking

Figuration

Beta-thinking

Today's
Vocabulary
WORD

Figuration

The most relevant to this discussion, figuration, describes how things become things.

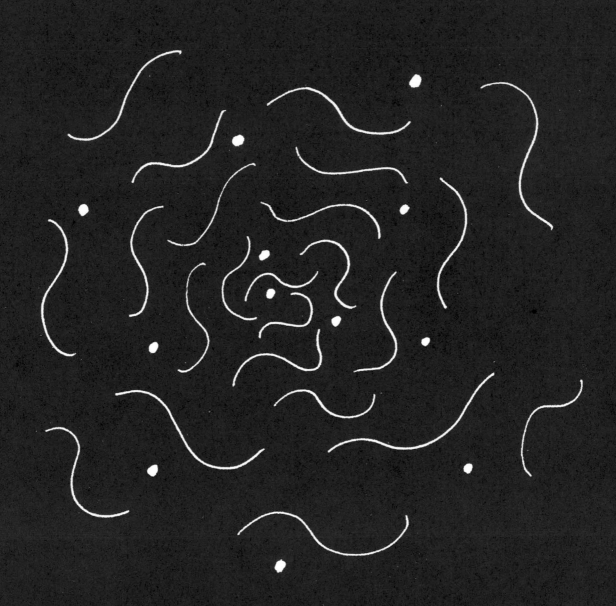

If we continue to develop the line
of reasoning begun on previous pages, we would
have to say that ONLY the waves are independent of
our sense apparatus, until the waves interact with
our sense apparatus to form particles.

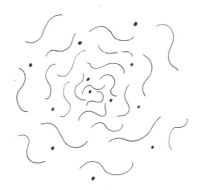

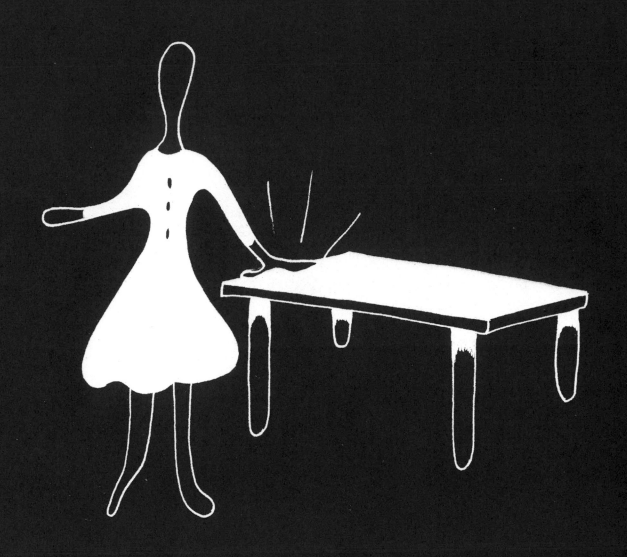

And so, in order for form to arise, "the sense-organs must be related to the particles in such a way as to give rise to sensations .... "*

* *Saving the Appearances: A Study in Idolatry*, Owen Barfield, Wesleyan University Press, 1988, page 24.

Also, "… those mere sensations must be combined and constructed by the percipient mind into the recognizable and nameable objects we call 'things'."*

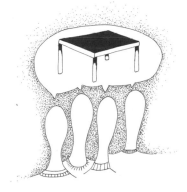

* *Saving the Appearances: A Study in Idolatry*, Owen Barfield, Wesleyan University Press, 1988, page 24.

Particles/Waves + Sensations + Mind = Figuration

It is this work of construction by
the mind that Barfield called figuration.

Particles/Waves + Sensations + Mind =
Figuration

Barfield used alpha-thinking to describe
how, after we have established objects in our world,
we can begin to think about them.

In the activity of thinking about, as well as in the process called figuration, we remain unconscious of the intimate relationship these things that we are thinking about have to our senses and to our minds.

In alpha-thinking we are even more unconscious than before, for our attitude is to treat things as completely independent from ourselves. We speculate about them or investigate them as originating outside ourselves. We study them in relationship to one another. Scientific thinking would be an example of this.

Beta-thinking is the kind of thinking that we are doing at this moment.

75

Beta-thinking is the domain of philosophy and psychology. With this kind of thinking we can consider the nature of our collective agreements.

The Collective
Agreement

We are almost ready to look at what happened about 500 years ago. First let us ask what our collective agreement was until that time. What was our relationship to objects long ago, before the printing press and the scientific revolution?

For the most part, wisdom and knowledge were passed down orally, through stories. The depth of abstract thought, the ability to objectify to the extent we do now, was not possible without the written word. People who read and write relate written words to the objects they describe, and also relate written words to each other. They forget that the object they read about has real substance. They are bound up in thoughts and ideas, not real things. They can mentally take part in experiences without participating. That is drastically different from knowing only the sounds of words.

I t would be difficult to do what we are
doing at this very moment without the technology
of the written word. Our collective agreement now is based
on it. You and I could not interact as we do without it
(beta-thinking). Nor could we do scientific research without
the objective memory it provides (alpha-thinking). Since
recorded history began, people have used the written word to
think about themselves and their environment. However,
that did not become the foundation of the collective
agreement until most people could read and write,
and therefore had access to this tool for thinking.

This written word, this TOOL for thinking, does something more. It enables us to participate with words and our imagination without participating with objects themselves. And that brings us to what our collective agreement was 500 years ago and back through history as far as we can go.

two Sides of the Same Coin

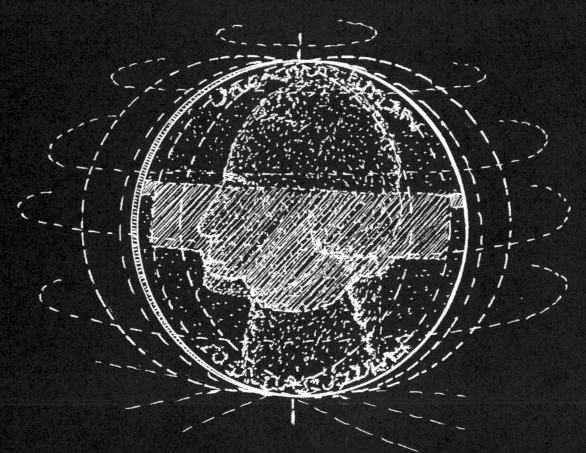

Our collective agreement in the past
was not abstract as it is today. It was PARTICIPATORY,
meaning that there was little difference between our
subjective and objective worlds. Our subjective and
objective worlds were a united whole.

two Sides of the Same Coin

We saw the ground of our own being, and the soul of everything—forms, objects, all of nature— as one united whole. Everything was part of everything else, all acting on and influencing one another. We could only view the world in that way because the ability—this THINKING TOOL—that has enabled us to separate and abstract ourselves from our ground of being, was not in place yet. The written word had not yet been COLLECTIVELY experienced. It was not yet our Western basis for the measurement of truth.

Remember reading earlier that when an
old paradigm passes away, it is almost impossible to
access it? At this point, I think we need to try. It won't
be easy and it needs contemplation. But using our
imagination to its fullest, let's see if we can put
ourselves for a moment into the shoes of an ordinary
medieval man, and think the habitual thoughts
common to his paradigm.

As a medieval man, you would not spend much time thinking analytically. Imagine standing on an outcropping overlooking the sea, simply aware that you are looking at one of the four elements of which all things on earth, including your body, are composed.

fire — water

earth air

As that ordinary medieval man, experience
the element of water inwardly as one of the four humors
that make up your very temperament. Experience earth,
fire, water and air as living parts of yourself. You consider
the proper mixture of those humors essential to good
health as well as to good character.

In those times, you would have actually experienced earth, fire, water and air as living parts of yourself. You knew that those elements were also related to the stars, as were you, through the constellated signs of the Zodiac. You saw all of nature as alive, kindled by the same soul force that enlivened you. You saw yourself as equal with, not superior to, all of nature.

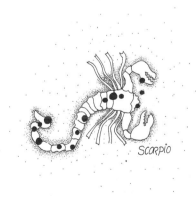

scorpio

If you had struck a bargain, cut a finger or lost a farm tool, you would have viewed the event, no matter how minor, as intertwined with the whole cosmos. Whatever happened was a sign of your own condition within the whole continuum—that included heaven and earth and all of creation.

Although this example is only a small taste of how medieval man experienced his life, at least it gives us a glimpse of how different the collective agreement was then from ours today. Unlike what we do today, medieval man, and all mankind before him, fully experienced being part of the environment and participating with it.

Our Present Collective

B ut, have we really stopped participating
with our environment? Haven't we seen that FORM
itself depends on PARTICIPATION of the senses with
the environment, beginning at the level of the
very tiny, with waves and particles?

We have also seen how the collective
agreement gives shape and context to these
forms, even deciding what they will BE
by way of focus and attention.

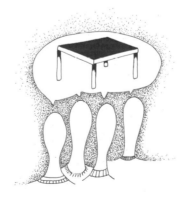

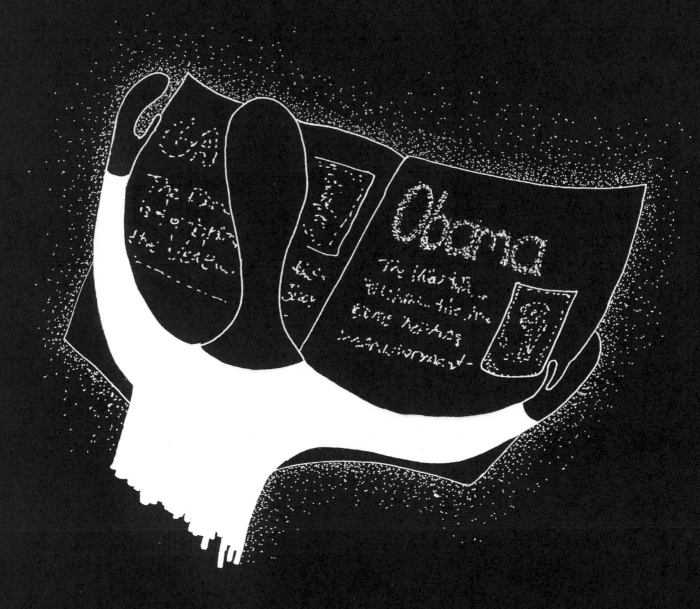

Today the great majority of us know
how to read. Instead of PARTICIPATING
consciously with the four elements as did medieval
man, we have refocused our attention into a profound
PARTICIPATION "with inked marks upon a page."*

*The Spell of the Sensuous, David Abram, Vintage Books, 1997, page 131.

The spread of literacy—conscious participation among many people with the written word, provided the foundation needed to give rise to the scientific revolution, and to our present collective agreement that is based upon it.

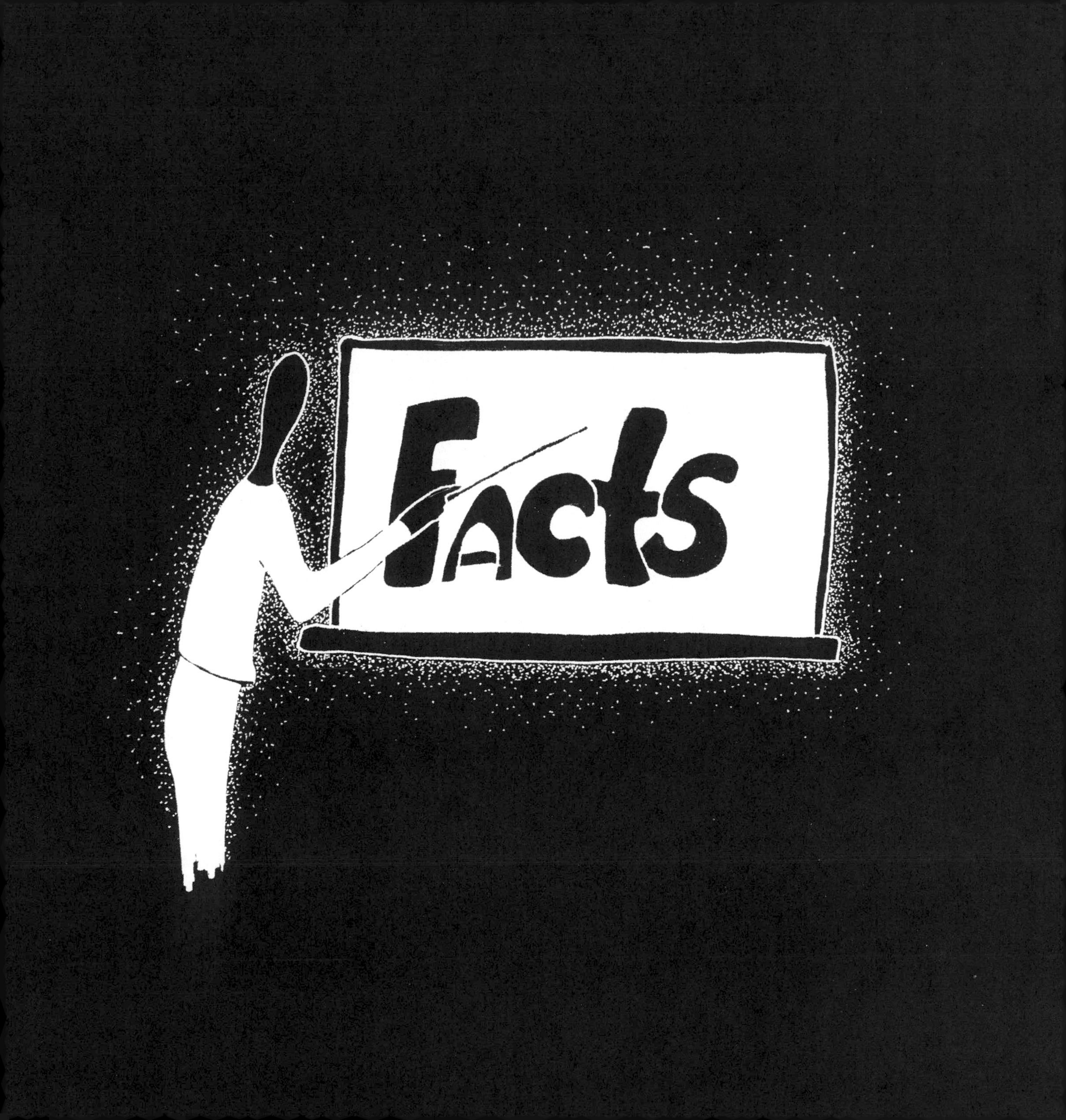
Facts

Once we could COLLECTIVELY remove ourselves from our environment, that became our paradigm, and all of us began to examine everything objectively. That process of examination itself has become our present collective agreement. In other words, scientific study has become our test of truth.

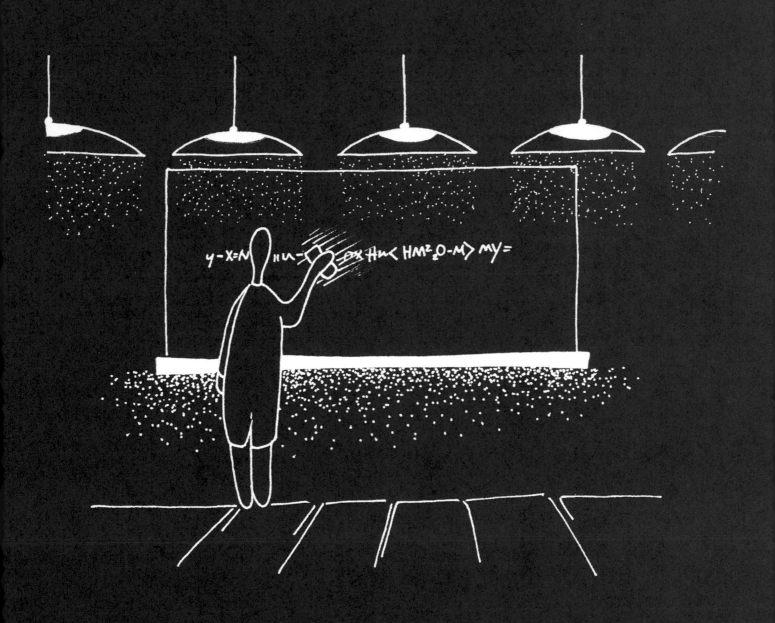

Comparatively, our collective agreement
is still young. And we are just beginning, with
the advent of quantum physics, to get a glimpse
of what we have REALLY been studying
for the past 500 years.

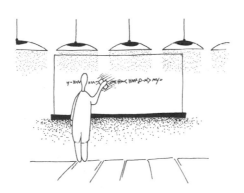

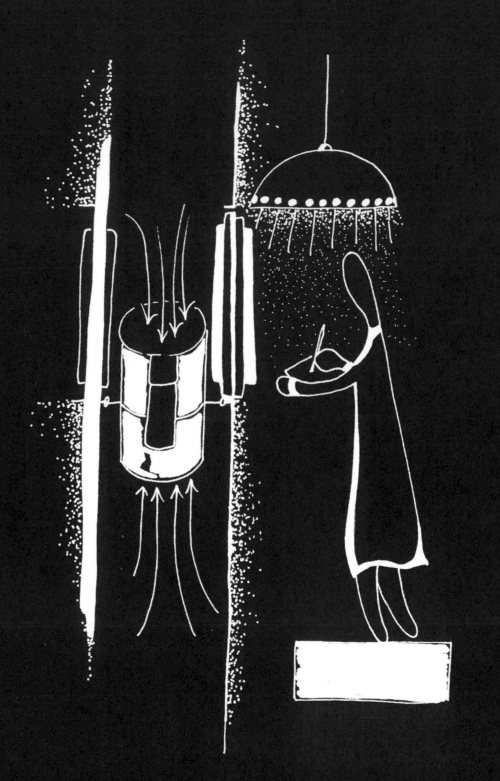

We have not been studying ALL of our human history up till now. What we have been studying is ONLY our PRESENT collective agreement. In other words, what we are beginning to see due to quantum physics is the representational nature of our collective agreements. Our tangible world represents our collective agreements—really just particles interacting with our sense apparatus that are then given context in accordance with those same agreements.

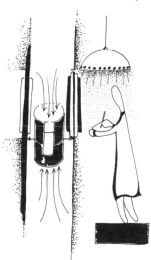

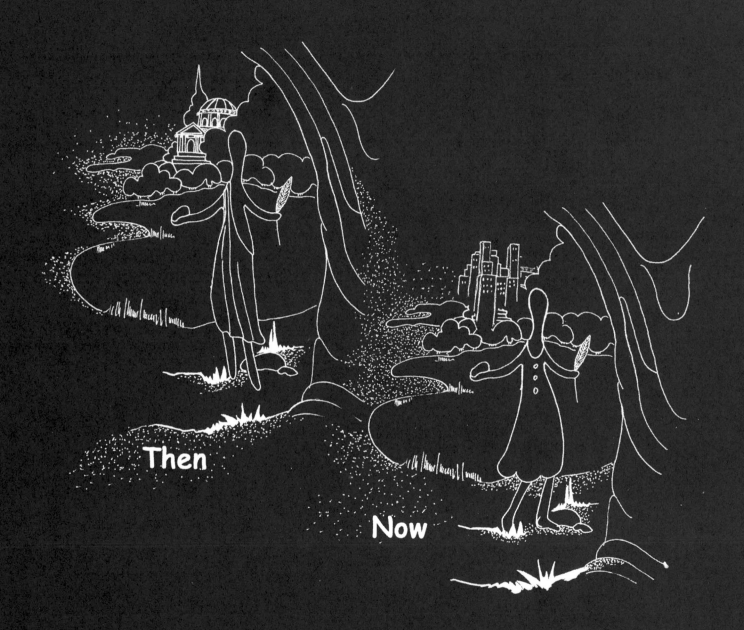

Our present 'representational' collective agreement is based on our scientific outlook. This outlook, combined with our agreement, has us believing that objects and forms are static, and have always been a constant, never-changing reality. Most of us believe that this reality is basically solid and separate and therefore can be studied completely objectively. We believe that objective study, in fact, is how truth is discovered—the scientific method.

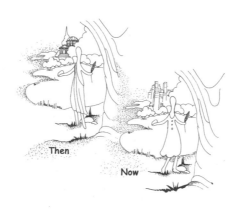

Now, TECHNICALLY, science has enabled
us to see how we create all collective agreements and
the figurations that support them. Science has shown
us that we have created our particular current collective
agreement and that this agreement is only one possibility
among infinite possibilities. Even though our present
collective agreement is the fertile ground out of
which these discoveries have sprung, this present
agreement itself hides from us the real truth of
those very same discoveries.

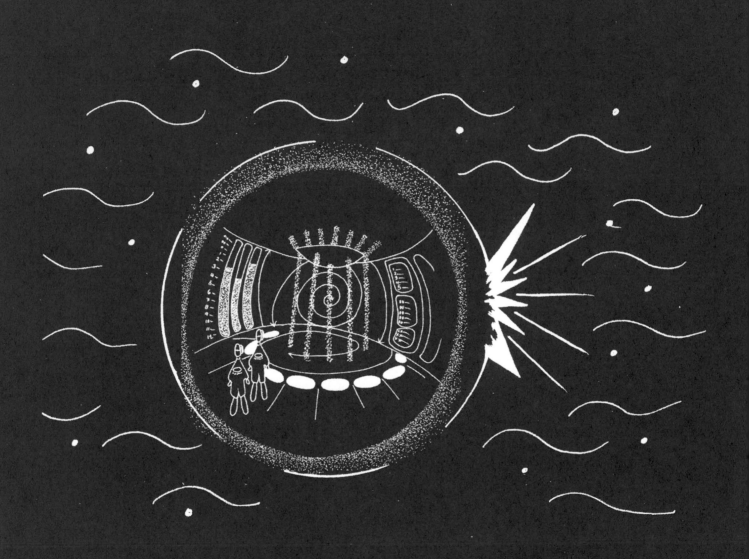

What is the truth? The truth is simply that we have been studying our own creation, our own figuration, and our own collective agreement as though we had nothing to do with its existence. In fact, we have gotten so technically proficient, so scientifically advanced, that we actually broke through our present figuration to the 'stuff' that makes all figuration possible. It is that deeper realm that quantum physics addresses. Yet, for the most part, we don't fully realize what that deeper realm—that 'stuff'—is.

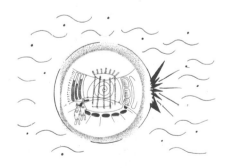

Intelligence

And what is that 'stuff'? It is Infinite Potential. It is Intelligence. It is Unfragmented Wholeness, and it is Awareness. It is the foundation of all figurations, and is that in which all figurations reside. We could call IT the PRINCIPLE of existence.

Why can't we see this? Why does our present agreement hide the truth? It hides it for the same reason that we can't go back and see the world through our ancestors' eyes. Because all agreements, all figurations, all forms, by definition, have limits. Throughout history, all agreements changed and expanded as the old agreements (paradigms) became too limited. Our present agreement is too limited! We have outgrown it, as is obvious by the discoveries of the quantum world, to say nothing of the dilemmas of our daily lives.

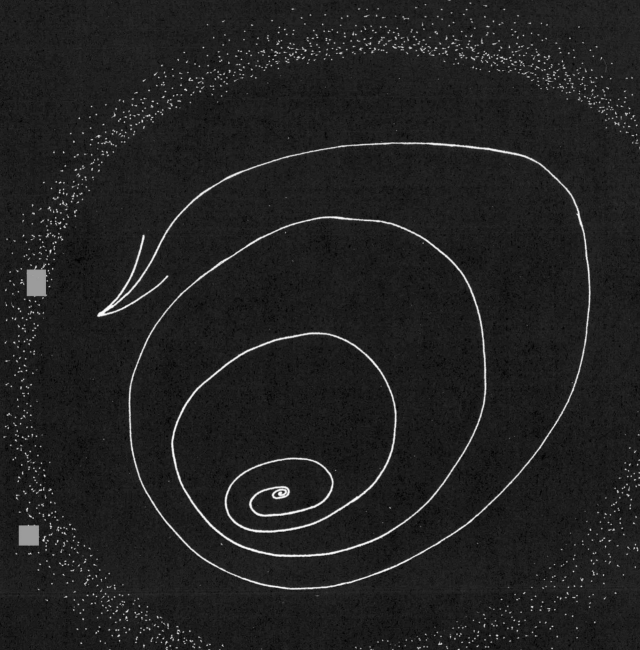

Like our ancestors who experienced the beginning of the scientific revolution, we are living at the time of a very big paradigm change. However, this time, the new paradigm will incorporate within it all of the previous paradigms. Why? Because our consciousness, our figurations, all our paradigms are one, ever continuous, expanding whole. And now, for the first time, we have the ability, even scientifically, to know that. Consciousness IS evolving and becoming more AWARE of itself. We are this AWARENESS, and now have the ability to see this evolution.

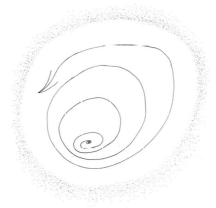

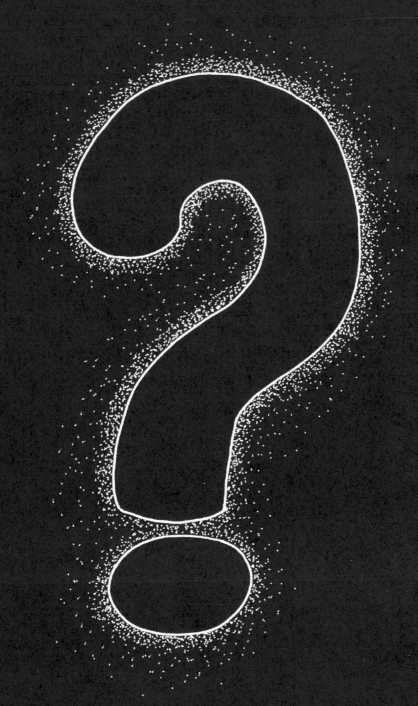

S O LET'S SPECULATE! As you and I and
all of us who make up this collective agreement,
begin to recognize the huge significance of what
we have been discussing here, what will happen?

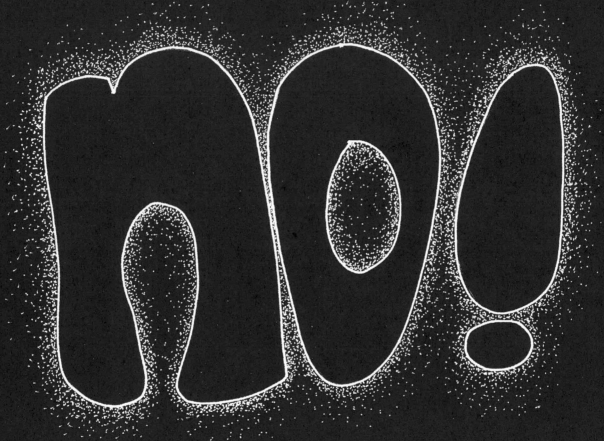

At the very foundation of our present collective view is our perception of history. This will radically change. All collective agreements, including our present one, depend on our figuration of waves/particles into objects. That is because of the intimate relationship between those particles and our senses and our minds. If that is so, can we really view the objects in our historical past accurately using our present collective agreement? Are those objects static and unchanging? In other words, can the phenomenal world ever really be studied historically, or even objectively? Obviously, the answer is NO!

Does this mean that we can't study history?
No, of course not. But we can't study the history of objects, because all that we ever really study is our present (about to change) collective agreement. What we can study historically is the evolution of our collective views, and how that evolution is allowing us to become more conscious of what our beings really are. Our consciousness is Infinite Potential, Intelligence, Unfragmented Wholeness and Awareness, ever becoming more aware of itself.

137

Can we end here, and just leave it at this?
We cannot, since we may not survive, historically or otherwise, if we don't change our present approach— to our planet and to ourselves. Many of us are actively engaged in raising human understanding to a level that will divert the disasters of global warming and other catastrophes that would leave our earth uninhabitable. Our huge misunderstanding about who we are affects every single area of life on this planet. Therefore in Volume 3 we will take a further look at who we are, where we are and where, perhaps, we should be by now.

THANK YOU

I must thank my family members for their loving support
and understanding as the writing, illustrating and publishing
of these little books unfolded. Special thanks go to my
husband for his patience when deadlines
consumed my energy.

Terry with her son

When the author, Terry Favour, first asked the question "Who Are We?" her very ability to form such thoughts and sentences was just beginning. The failure of those around her to answer back, set her on a quest that would last indefinitely. The process led her across a diversified terrain, weaving back and forth through spiritual philosophy and science, from East to West.

As an adult she has sustained herself and this passion working as an artist and designer, owning and operating a small ethnic arts company with her son, located in Northern New Mexico. In the 1980s she became interested in the Enneagram. In 2004 she and her daughter studied under David Daniels and Helen Palmer and they both became certified Enneagram teachers.

She feels that expanding one's limitations should be an unending endeavor so she continues this life work every day. It was her grown children who led her to write these three little books, stating that she had a knack for simplifying complicated matters.

She continues to draw and write and she lives in Santa Fe NM with her husband and her cat.